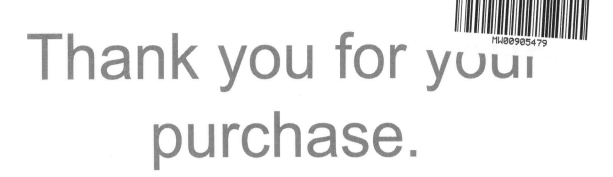
# Thank you for your purchase.

We hope you enjoy colouring these patterns as much as we do!

## Now claim your free bonus at

## www.colorwithkim.com/amazon

Download 20 free adult colouring patterns - perfect for printing and colouring at home, as many times as you like!

Plus exclusive news, updates and more coloring goodies at colorwithkim.com

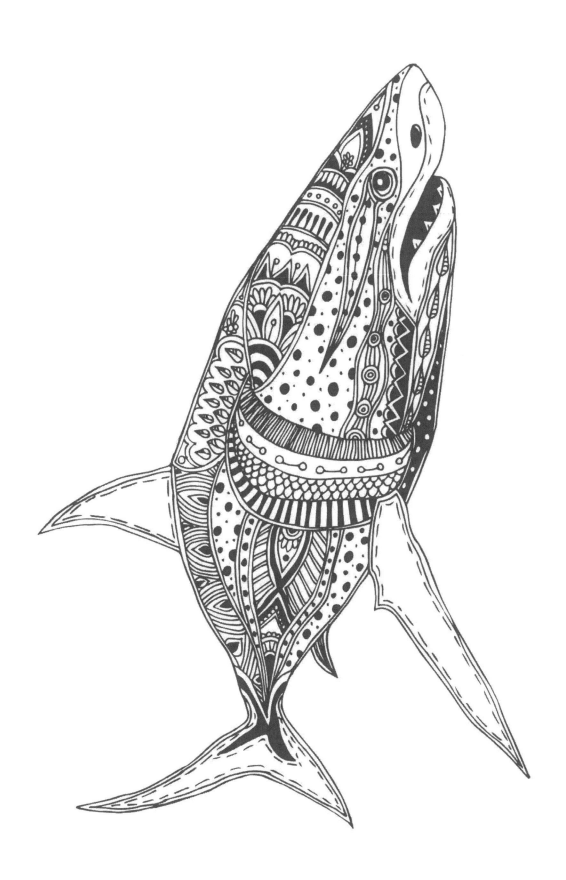

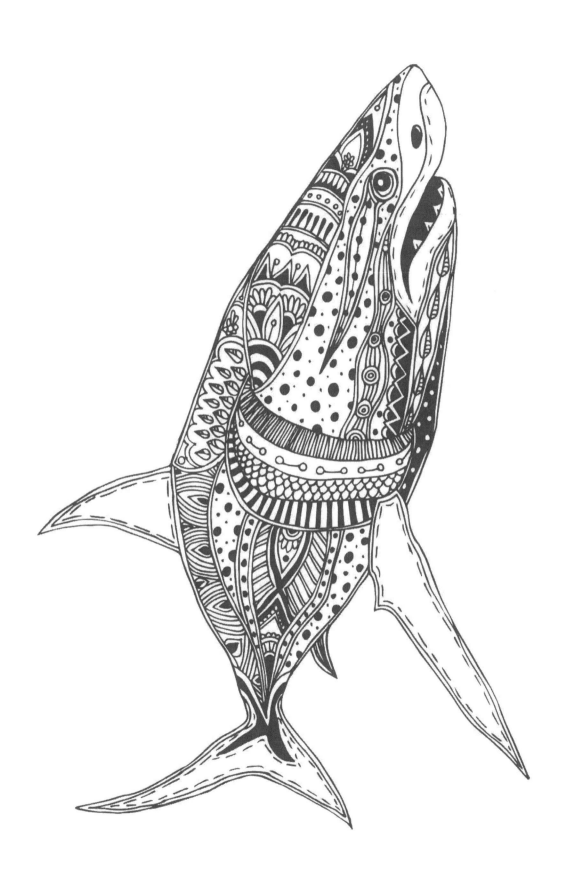

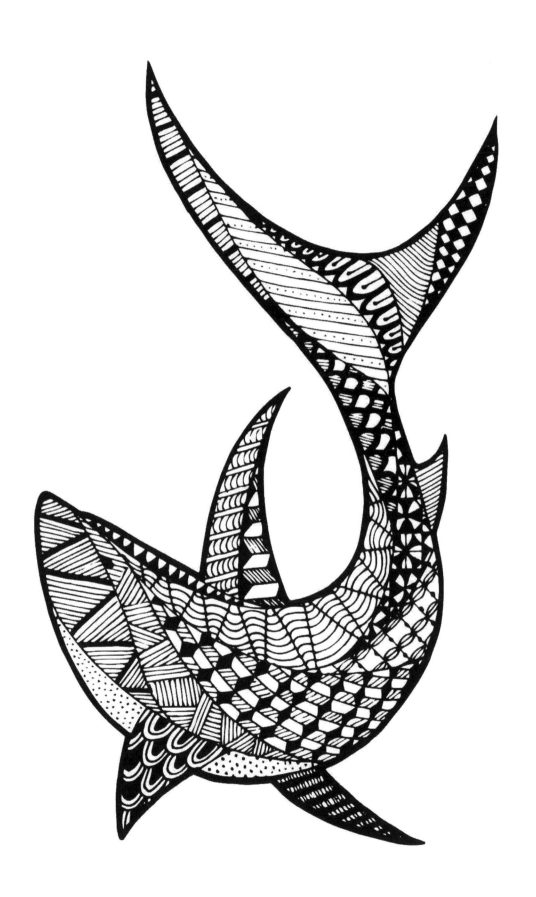

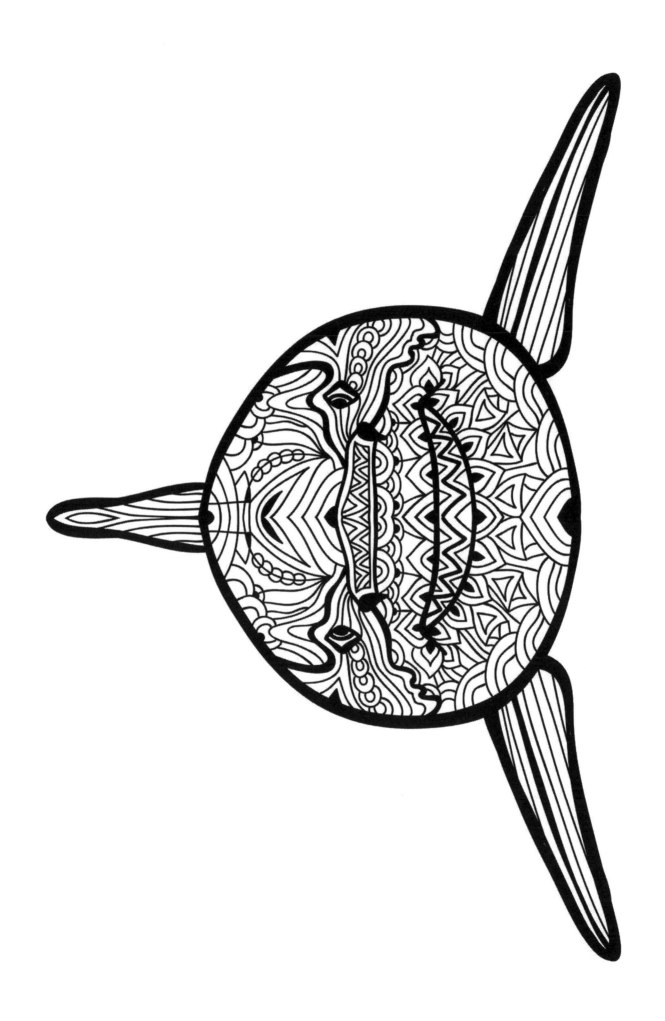

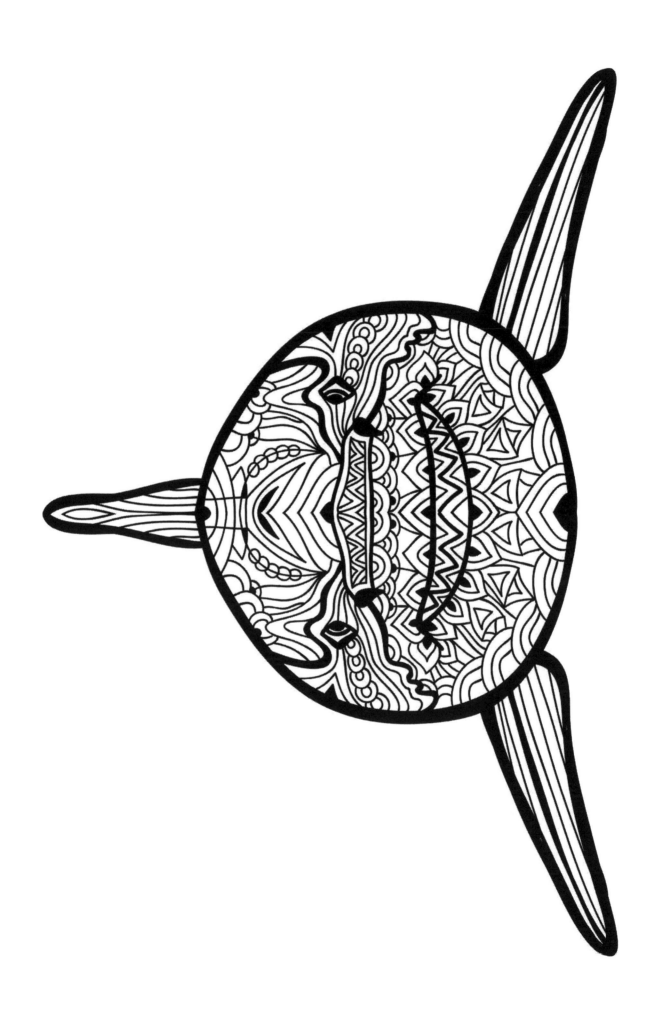

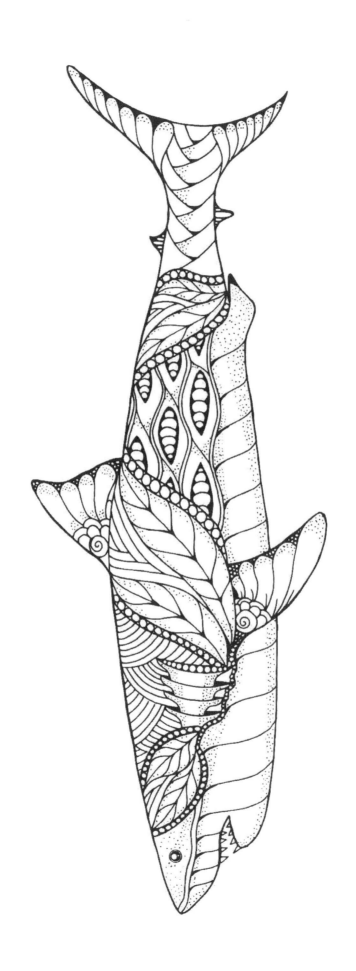

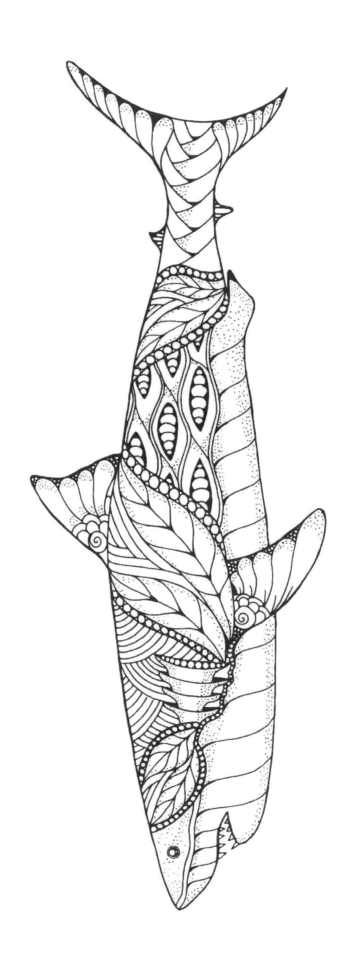

Made in the USA
Middletown, DE
30 November 2020